My name is Dan Wel

www.AirbnbHell.com. I launched the website in July
of 2013 after I personally experienced a loss of
almost $3,000 US dollars due to the senseless and
unfair policies of Airbnb, as well as the incompetence
of a series of Airbnb customer service agents. Inside
this book you'll hear stories from a number of guests
and hosts, including myself.

Our goal as a community is not to whine without
reason, but rather to warn other potential hosts and
guests about the dangers and risks associated with
using the Airbnb service specifically. Some of our
authors hate the "sharing economy" concept in
general, but I personally think it's a great thing to be
able to rent out my extra bedrooms for additional
income, and I've personally continued as both a host
and guest using other services such as VRBO and
HomeAway. In fact, we have an entire page dedicated
to the many reputable companies cropping up all over
the world to compete with Airbnb, you may view it
here: http://www.airbnbhell.com/airbnb-competitors.
Which specific home sharing company will win in the
long run is yet to be seen, but from my own
experience, I sincerely doubt it will be Airbnb.

Looking at the larger picture, it seems fairly obvious
to me that society is moving more and more in the
direction of shared resources. Shared homes and
vehicles are just the beginning in my opinion. One
might ask, "what will happen if this trend continues to

a point where virtually no one actually owns property and everyone prefers to travel around and rent each other's homes?" On the one hand, there is certainly a strong argument stating that when people do not own the space where they live, they generally do not take very good care of it compared to homeowners. This can be seen in virtually any apartment complex in the world. There is a reason why most landlords require significant security deposits in advance, it's because they know there is a very good chance that the tenant will not leave their space in the same condition in which they found it. Most homeowners not only take more pride in their property, but many of them also understand the direct financial incentive of keeping their property in good condition so it appreciates over time and they can eventually reap those rewards if/when they or their heirs sell the property. On the other hand, this problem of "neglectful tenants" can and has been relatively well addressed by the implementation of security deposits. I see no reason why this logic would not or could not continue on a larger scale within the modern "sharing economy" so long as the exchange of funds is handled either directly between the landlord and tenant, or is handled professionally by a dedicated and ethical 3rd party company.

In other words, Airbnb's CONCEPT is great, but their execution, company culture, and individual policies leave much to be desired. These problems are solve-able, and I'm sincerely optimistic that sooner or later a better company will rise up and crush Airbnb, much like Facebook crushed MySpace. Right now the world likes Airbnb because they were the first to take the sharing economy concept to large-scale, but unless they make significant changes to their policies and corporate culture, they'll soon be replaced by one of their more worthy competitors (http://www.airbnbhell.com/airbnb-competitors).

Thank you for taking an interest in this issue, and for supporting our community. Together we will create a safer and more pleasant residence sharing environment for all!

Dan Weber
Founder, Airbnb Hell

OVERVIEW

"...I believe that Airbnb is providing a great service, but this is an issue they need to address. They are very strict about renter cancellations, but to my knowledge, no penalty befell our host for canceling less than 24 hours in advance, besides a warning."
Last Minute Cancellation, Airbnb Hell

In many ways, Airbnb represents a reflection of society. No matter how civilized we consider ourselves, there are always going to be outliers who bend the rules, some with low levels of awareness who play loud music in public, and others who openly discriminate and threaten violence against those who challenge their backward beliefs.

In the course of writing this book, I've had the chance

to read hundreds of submissions through the AirbnbHell.com site, horror stories in the news involving cases of racial discrimination, sexual harassment, assault, and even murder, and viral videos documenting damage to one's home so thorough and destructive it seems impossible for one person to have committed it in one night. We will of course be sharing these submissions, but not to come off as one-sided, wagging our fingers at Airbnb and shouting "shame, shame, shame!"

Rather, we want you to be aware. Despite all the controversy in the news surrounding Airbnb, there are still millions of people who swear by it. The idea is sound: hosts benefit by getting a little extra cash for renting a spare bedroom, or when they're out of their houses for the holidays or traveling for work, and guests find comfort in accommodations with an actual kitchen, furniture, and sense of home. However, as Airbnb users may be aware, the website has been infiltrated with landlords who kick out long-term tenants to make a profit on short-term renters, scam artists who put up fake listings to con travelers into sending them money outside of the platform, an Airbnb customer service department woefully inadequate for thousands often needing immediate assistance, and, as in the story above, hosts who cancel on guests at the last minute, often facing no financial penalties and no incentive to stop[1].

---

[1] Poston, Ben. "L.A. Apartment Owners Charged with Allegedly Evicting Tenants, Then Renting Their Units via Airbnb." Los Angeles Times. 20 June 2016. <http://www.latimes.com/local/california/la-me-ln-landlords-illegal-rentals-20160620-snap-story.html>

This book is designed to help all Airbnb users. Not just to become better guests and hosts, but to keep their eyes open to the problems the platform has allowed to happen through inaction. The first step is to read the Airbnb Terms and Conditions and recognize that if you use the Airbnb platform, you have virtually no rights or recourse in the event of any dispute. After that, keep reading this book for more practical examples and advice!

Table of Contents

SECTION I: GUESTS

CHAPTER ONE: If any of your personal items, cash, or valuables are stolen (by the host, guests, or burglars) you have no protection from Airbnb.

> *"...while staying at an Airbnb in Pasadena and looking for a permanent place, our apartment got broken into and everything we had brought with us including our passports, birth certificates, national ID cards, all our academic diplomas and transcripts, and every single immigration document we had got stolen (including the copies of them)... Financial loss is something that you can forget and recover from, however the loss of all identification documents, educational records, and most importantly the feeling of having been violated this way, is something that will be haunting us for a long time."*
> <u>Lost Everything in Airbnb Theft... Inside Job?</u>,
> Airbnb Hell

Theft can happen in any country, in any situation. Airbnb hosts and guests are subject to local laws while using the service, but the business model as a whole isn't designed to protect either in the event of theft. Airbnb touts a "one million dollar insurance policy' as its way of protecting hosts, but as they say on their own site, this does not cover cash and many valuables[2]. Though it's true many chain hotels do not assume liability if valuables are stolen, there are more checks and balances in place:

- Many mid-range hotels and above offer in-room safes
- Hotel keycards are voided after a guest's stay, whereas Airbnb guests can potentially copy keys from past stays and retain them for future use
- While surveillance and security are largely

---

[2] The $1,000,000 Host Guarantee. Airbnb. <https://www.airbnb.com/guarantee>.

absent from people's homes, hotels usually

have at least one camera and possibly guards

As the guest in the story above came to realize, it's

entirely possible her Airbnb hosts were negligent in

giving out easily copied keys to guests or completely

culpable by disguising their home as a safe

environment, then burgling the place themselves

while the guests were out.

**What can hosts and guests do to protect
themselves?**

Guests can take some steps to help protect themselves

prior to booking a reservation by messaging potential

hosts and asking them about the security of their

home, especially regarding how access is granted to

new guests (simply passing an easily duplicated

physical key from one guest to another, or using a more secure passcode combination lock with a new passcode for each guest).

Since Hosts also have problems with theft from guests, many hosts have tried locking or even sealing off a separate room to which guests would not have a key, but with unrestricted access to their house for a number of days, breaking in wouldn't be too difficult. As Airbnb suggests, a separate insurance policy for your personal items – computer, jewelry, etc. – is certainly better than filing a claim with the Airbnb customer service department and hoping for compensation.

> *"They stole all of our furniture, washer, dryer, artwork, and dishes. We immediately contacted Airbnb, filed a police report, found our receipts and emailed them all to Airbnb. They have done nothing to take care of this. They have a million*

dollar insurance policy and we never received a dime from this theft. Their insurance guy won't return our phone calls and so we lost $15,000 worth of furnishings and appliances and Airbnb has done nothing to help us."
<u>Airbnb Allows Theft and Does Nothing</u>, Airbnb Hell

The only way to completely ensure your belongings will be safe may be to simply keep them off the property. For hosts, this means asking a friend or neighbor to store a few things while a guest rents the listing. For guests, consider minimizing what you leave behind in an Airbnb property while you're out sightseeing or working; ask yourself if anything is irreplaceable. If it is, don't let it out of your sight.

> *"Before they arrived I put a lock on my bedroom door because I wasn't going to be there while they were staying and let's be honest – I didn't know them from a bar of soap. So call me naive, but I assumed that a lock would be a clear indication that I didn't want them in my room. They had two rooms to choose from, there*

15

was no need for them to go into mine. Obviously the lock made no difference because it's quite easy to just unscrew the hinges and take the door off! All of my personal belongings got rummaged through, my lingerie was all over the bed and sentimental jewelry items were stolen that can never be replaced. Airbnb's response when I reported the situation? "You shouldn't leave your belongings out if you don't want them tampered with."

Don't host on airbnb!!!, Airbnb Hell

CHAPTER TWO: If there is a foul odor, loud noises, or any other problems with your room that are not easily documented with photos, you are out of luck and your claim for a refund will be denied.

> *"The bed linen was so old and musty it made us feel sick. The carpets were dark brown, covering a multitude of sins, but they were clearly very old and smelly. At one point I decided to get closer for a sniff – the smell of old feet and dirt was quite overpowering. How the host could expect us to be happy about letting our 14-month old crawl over them is beyond me! And the smell from under the bath was just as bad – years of accumulated dirt in a damp room led to a strong smell of stinky socks emanating from the area."*
>
> Shell Cottage? More like Smell Cottage!,
> Airbnb Hell

One of the main flaws in Airbnb's business model is the lack of staff. Of course, they have IT professionals who step if the site is in danger of crashing, but the entire company has fewer than 3000 people across the globe. A few thousand people to potentially handle **over 50 million** Airbnb users if a host doesn't show up; if there are charges of sexual harassment; if the property simply isn't there; and if a guest arrives to find the host living in squalor, the bed covered in insects or the whole room looking like it hasn't been dusted in years.

Obviously, there are different standards of cleanliness people maintain in their own homes. A university student who has been used to living in close quarters with three other people might be jubilant having an Airbnb room to herself on holiday, even if there's a bit of mold and the sheets have holes in them; such a stay might earn her host positive feedback. Whereas a working professional, seeing the reviews, would book the room and be absolutely

18

appalled at the lack of care. So who is right?

There's a reason hotels, restaurants, and many businesses open to the public are graded accordingly to their tidiness and hygiene. Although there might be millions of people who wouldn't know the difference if they entered a room crawling with bugs or one completely sterilized on a nightly basis, those in the hospitality industry know there's a certain standard from which to judge:

- Silence bothers no one; noise can drive some people insane
- Odors and smells can go overlooked, but why take the chance?
- Cleanliness is next to godliness, in all things

The bottom line is: when Airbnb hosts don't meet these standards, do you have any recourse, with ner service, local authorities, or an agency like

the Better Business Bureau?

> *"The kitchen smelled like rotting vegetables. The stove needed to be lit with a grill lighter and the only available utensils and cookware were covered in food. There was a load of laundry in the washing machine. We were left with two towels for a 5-day stay, one of which had a giant hole in it. The sheets provided had a small blood stain on them. The apartment was also quite noisy. The noise ranged from being able to hear a neighbor's cell phone vibrating on the floor above us to hobos screaming down the street at 3AM."*
> <u>Smelly, loud, and dirty. A terrible place to stay in Paris</u>, Airbnb Hell

What can guests do to get a full or partial refund?

If you were in a chain hotel and arrived to find

your room smelling like rotten eggs, you'd have

several options available to you. First you would

address the front desk staff. If that didn't work, you

could reach out to their corporate overlords. If there's

still no resolution, vent your frustrations to social media and online reviews; the thought of bad publicity spreading is enough to get the company to provide a refund or some form of compensation.

With Airbnb, however, it's not so cut and dried. Merely saying there was excessive noise or pungent smells isn't enough to satisfy the resolution center: do you have proof? There are a few ways to go about this. Before you even attempt to get a refund or partial refund, document everything. As a guest, if you have the slightest bit of doubt about the quality of your Airbnb or the amenability of your host, it's best to get everything in writing or something customer service can actually see if and when a problem does arise. To that end, restrict all communication to Airbnb's messaging system; customer service has previously rejected screenshots of texts and WhatsApp messages between guests and hosts as proof of violation of the terms of use, and obviously not many people record their calls. When you arrive at the property, pull out your camera and be the biggest shutterbug you can: record the state of the Airbnb at the moment you arrive and the moment you leave, to ensure no claims can be made for property damage.

This may help with issues like cleanliness and claims of theft, but what about annoying smells and sounds? If they are so unbearable you need to leave the property, the simplest way is to address the host through the Airbnb messaging service and ask for a refund. The problem may be with their property, but that doesn't mean they're beyond reason with a polite request and explanation. Even if they say no, the goal is to get them to acknowledge an intangible problem for future claims to customer service, e.g. "Yeah, that smell has been there for years, but no guest has complained before."

Should they refuse a refund and deny the problem exists, it's highly unlikely the Airbnb resolution center will rule in the guest's favor:

> *"This was my first experience with Airbnb, traveling with my sisters and daughter to New York City. We thought renting an Airbnb so everyone could have their own rooms would be a great idea. The host would not give us the exact address until three days prior to our stay, yet her refund policy was strict: no refund for a cancellation within seven days of a stay. The reviews on this Airbnb were all positive and there was no mention of noise from a water bottle distributor under the apartment windows... until two months prior to my stay. I have stayed in many cities (none using Airbnb) and know that they can be noisy, but all four of us felt like we were sleeping on the streets that night. To top it off, the water bottle distributor*

began operations at 4:00 AM, with forklifts going forward and backwards (including beeping) from then throughout the morning. No one in my party received more than a few hours of sleep that night. So as not to ruin our entire vacation we contacted the host and said we could not stay because of the noise, which was not mentioned anywhere in her post. The host would not negotiate any refund whatsoever. In order to save our vacation and get some sleep we were forced to vacate and move to a hotel for the remaining three nights of our New York trip. My next step was to contact Airbnb. They took my comments and I sent some photos of the window air conditioner that had openings to the outdoors and the street view of the water bottling company next door. After a brief review of the situation, Airbnb denied my request for three nights' reimbursement. In a hotel one has the ability to change rooms if one isn't satisfactory. There is no such option with an Airbnb. I will never use Airbnb again."
Distributor Kept us Awake in this Loud NYC Airbnb. Airbnb Hell

Reaching out to Airbnb through social media - Facebook and Twitter - is sometimes effective, but still putting messages out into the ether rather than contacting one specific person who might be capable of help. One Airbnb guest found a rather

ingenious solution to this problem, by searching

LinkedIn:

> *"We had a pretty horrendous situation with a host, drug use in our flat, and a three-month booking. Customer service was absolutely hopeless. We moved to a hotel because we had to leave the property immediately and Airbnb was refusing to pay for more than one night at a time. We were extremely stressed having just moved to a new country, started new jobs, and also had huge amounts of luggage with us too.*
>
> *It got to a point where we were getting absolutely nowhere after five or six days of being on the phone with them for six hours a day - they were refusing to refund us or rehome us - so I went onto LinkedIn, found Aisling Hassell (Head of Airbnb CX in Ireland), signed up to a free premium trial, and sent her a pretty desperate InMail message appealing to her to do something/explaining our situation. I left my name, number and booking reference. She got back in touch immediately - called us direct so we had her mobile number - and started to resolve the situation.*
>
> *We also got handed to Ian Watson in Singapore who is the Director of Customer Experience and*

Trust & Safety. These two people can actually make decisions (unlike the case managers it would seem) and it was the only reason we managed not to lose thousands of dollars and end up homeless. It was terrible that we had to resort to using channels outside Airbnb to talk to someone who could help, but it worked completely, and I would encourage people in such situations to browse LinkedIn and send out messages to senior people in the company."

(Name withheld by request)

CHAPTER THREE: If you rent a single room, there is no guarantee regarding how many people might be living in a given home/condo while you are there. If there is a shared bathroom, you might end up sharing it with 1 person, or 20.

> *"[The host] didn't tell me the bathroom would also be shared with any transient she could shove into any space she had. She tried to make it out to be some hippie idea of communal living, but her real colours showed when it came time for money. She is very much in this to try to squeeze as much out of unsuspecting renters as she can. I'm not exaggerating when I say she rents out every place she can: all the bedrooms, the basement, the shed in the backyard (for real), and a grungy algae-covered camping trailer in the driveway. And all these people use the same bathroom."*
> Airbnb Nightmare: Transient Hippie Flophouse,
> Airbnb Hell

Airbnb may have started as a way to rent out

entire houses and apartments while the owners were

on vacation, but it quickly transformed into something else. Those with the means signed multiple leases in high traffic areas to earn a profit on the rent, and it didn't take too long before hosts realized they could convert a home from a comfortable vacation rental for a couple to a crowded dormitory for a dozen people[3].

> *"I live in an apartment block in a now very hip part of Berlin. On the ground floor a family of four used to live in the apartment. They were pressured by their landlord to move out because he wanted to sell the property. The new owners claimed they would move in themselves. Instead they installed twelve beds in four rooms and have converted the apartment into a hostel which they list on Airbnb. That's twelve people staying in an apartment meant for a family of four to five people with guests changing every three to four days. Our children can no longer play in the courtyard unsupervised and our*

[3] "Airbnb in San Francisco: By The Numbers." Airbnb Citizen. N.p., 20 Sept. 2016. Web. <https://san-francisco.airbnbcitizen.com/airbnb-in-san-francisco-by-the-numbers/>.

privacy has been violated. Of course, the hosts of this hostel never asked the residents in the apartment if they were ok with any of this, and they deny what they are doing. This leaves us to have to prove to the authorities that there is a hostel being run in our house which is taking up time we would rather spend doing other things."
<u>Airbnb Hostel in our house</u>, Airbnb Hell

Although many of these properties are listed as is, there are quite a few hosts advertising private rooms without providing the whole picture. Let's say you do find a listing on the website that looks perfect for your situation: family home in the suburbs, private room, furnished common areas. Whether it's a hotel or an Airbnb, you need to be careful and judge the rental based on what you **can't** see, and isn't legally required to be mentioned, for example: proximity to a train track in service; downwind from a sewage treatment plant; or the fact that there are 20 residents in the 5-bedroom house who will be sharing the kitchen and living room, coming and going at different hours, and commandeering the shower when they see fit.

What can guests do to make sure they have enough space?

No matter what goes wrong when you stay at an Airbnb, contact customer service within 24 hours or they will claim there's nothing they can do due to company policy.

> "I booked an Airbnb unit in China, a simple one-bedroom entire home/apt. When I showed up, I had (surprise) eight roommates, no lock on my bedroom door, and cockroaches and trash everywhere. The house was maintained like the worst college dorm you could imagine. I left immediately and Airbnb refused to refund me because I didn't call them in the first 24 hours (try traveling to mainland china and using your mobile phone). Their slumlord host (who has my bad review and several other bad reviews in Chinese) is able to keep scamming unlucky

Airbnb customers and Airbnb keeps their fees and listings. Translate reviews. Don't trust Airbnb."

Scamming Slumlord in China Protected by Airbnb, Airbnb Hell

Unfortunately, there's very little that can be done if you're already checked into the Airbnb and didn't make prior inquiries. The best course of action is research and getting specific answers from the host. If the listing doesn't mention other people staying on the property, that isn't grounds for a refund in Airbnb's eyes, as long as your room is as described. On the other hand, if you take the time to send a message to the host asking how many residents will be sharing the unit and you discover he lied at check in, then the resolution center has something to work with. You should also ask the host prior to booking if there are any known noises, irritating neighbors, or abnormal smells, etc.

CHAPTER FOUR: A "fully stocked kitchen" means very different things to different people. One pot, two dishes and a handful of silverware does not mean you can actually cook a meal there, yet this is not enough evidence to seek a claim for refund.

> *"Two months before traveling to Chicago, I found a small apartment (in reality, the attic of an old Victorian) on Airbnb. I needed it for five nights and the description said there were three beds, a stocked kitchen, and a full bathroom. The price was right, so I booked it after exchanging emails with the host. In particular, I wanted to make sure it was safe and that I could prepare meals for my children... We flew into Chicago and arrived at the place. It was adorable. However, there was one bed... not three... The kitchen had a sink and a hot plate."*
> Airbnb Nightmare: Chicago Bait and Switch,
> Airbnb Hell

One of the biggest advantages to choosing an apartment or house rental over a hotel for a long stay is the convenience of cooking one's own food in a proper kitchen. For someone who has children, this is almost a necessity to ensure they eat healthily while away from home. Because very few hotels have fully stocked kitchens, wouldn't you think Airbnb hosts would be willing to provide such a service for guests?

There are two reasons why this may not always be the case. If you're renting a shared or private room in someone else's home and they're staying there during your booking, the kitchen may be full of pots, pans, dishes, and strainers, but you may not be allowed access as an Airbnb guest; under the amenities included on all Airbnb listings is an option for "space where guests can cook their own meals." It is the discretion of hosts as to whether guests can cook, and violating these rules is grounds for removal.

Expanding Airbnb users in major metropolitan areas like New York and Los Angeles has come with a lesson for the company in free enterprise. Namely, property owners have been known to remove long-term leaseholders in order to push up prices with short-term renters[4]. Morality of such a move aside, there's a reason why properties like these – i.e. those solely intended for Airbnb users – may be less appealing to prospective guests than an extra bedroom in someone's permanent home. Because landlords would now be in charge of furnishing and stocking everything from the bathroom to kitchen, some necessities simply go overlooked or ignored: spoons but no knives; a pasta strainer but no bowls. In

---

[4] Poston, Ben. "L.A. Apartment Owners Charged with Allegedly Evicting Tenants, Then Renting Their Units via Airbnb."

other words, an apartment or house furnished as cheaply as possible (resembling an IKEA showroom) to meet the minimum standards of Airbnb.

What can guests do to ensure hosts provide everything they listed?

There's obviously more at stake than a few items missing from a kitchen. What if a host's listing shows a TV, and you arrive to find it's not connected to anything? A bathroom with no soap or towels? A bed with no sheets or blankets during a winter stay?

> *"I had never used Airbnb before, but friends had said positive things about their experiences. I wanted a studio apartment, furnished, for a month in Strasbourg, France, while I house-hunted and decided on my future. I reserved a furnished studio. I knew the location. The host accepted the reservation, and Airbnb took my money.*

The host then called me to say she wanted to cancel as there was no bed in the apartment (why didn't she know this before?) – this was while I was on my way to meet her at the apartment to get the keys! I couldn't afford to wait for a refund and pay another rental at the same time. In any case I had to stay three nights in a hotel while waiting for the bed, which the host then decided could not be delivered for another two weeks (I could have gone to IKEA and bought a sofa bed the same afternoon in her place). At this point she offered me a 200€ refund, which I accepted, being otherwise homeless and already having spent a bunch of money I hadn't budgeted for.

The description said the place had basic kitchen items, but there was no plate, cup, saucepan, cutlery – nothing. I had to buy all that, as well as all the bed linen. Towels too."
 Supposedly furnished studio was not furnished!,
Airbnb Hell

This is the difference between the "good" hosts

Airbnb presents to the world – those who live in only

one house and truly do rent it out while on vacation –

and those who make up an increasing number of

users: those who use the platform as a business, owning more than one sparsely furnished property. While "good" Airbnb hosts would naturally have everything someone would want in a place to stay for a few days – bedding, towels, kitchen appliances, etc. – unscrupulous ones don't consider just how inconvenient their lack of furnishings may be to guests:

> *"What I booked, at the price of a 5-star hotel, for a weekend, was described as a beautiful downtown apartment, entirely for my use. It was actuality a third story walk up in an old, nasty building. There were no amenities or comforts provided; not even a spoon or fork in the kitchen, no chairs of any kind to sit on in any part of the so-called apartment, one shelf of refrigerator space, an unusable, old Keurig that leaked all over the counter and couldn't make a cup of coffee, a metal sign outside the window that creaked, banged and made racket all night in the wind, and a full size bed with what appeared to be twin sheets stretched over the rubber sheeted mattress that came off all night and made sleep impossible. This bed was in the*

middle of the one "furnished" room – that's all, just the bed; it had no bedspread, blanket or cover of any other kind. The host graciously left one newly purchased, never washed, Walmart towel for the entire weekend for 2 people."
Horrible Airbnb Experience for Overpriced

Stay, Airbnb Hell

In this case, very few guests have reported receiving refunds from Airbnb, even with photo evidence. The reason is hosts can change pictures on their listings between a guest's complaint and the response from customer service showing different properties and amenities that simply didn't exist during the guest's stay.

Because guests can't rely on the photos on the listing or even a host's promises through the Airbnb messaging system to ensure a refund when the property differs from the listing, the only course of action is a thorough walkthrough at check in, with pictures and videos timestamped to prove to Airbnb what was offered was different. Even so, once guests find there's something missing that they simply can't do without (a bed, perhaps?), they need to leave the property immediately and contact Airbnb within 24 hours, the sooner the better. While this may not always be possible for remote locations, staying even one night gives the host grounds to claim "it wasn't that bad if they stayed." Whether guests stay because they have no other options or leave because the property is lacking key amenities, getting a refund is still a shot in the dark.

CHAPTER FIVE: If the host or another guest has a party every night, you will have to thoroughly document each incident with video recordings and time stamps to seek any sort of claim or refund. Even then, it will be a battle that may take weeks and you are unlikely to win.

> *"My husband and I stayed in an absolutely gorgeous unit and for the first night it was lovely. It was when the second night came around that the problems started. The people that live above the unit we were staying in decided to have a party and at first we weren't too worried – we aren't that old, we understand the concept of fun. It was when it got to the third continuous day and night of partying that I thought I was going to lose my mind. We had two nights left of our stay and I rang Airbnb to see if there was anything they could do to arrange alternative accommodations because the party obviously wasn't stopping. They wanted me to prove that there had been constant noise. How silly of me! I should have known to record every second of the last 3 days to "prove" that there was noise. Or perhaps I could have run upstairs with my phone and asked the guys throwing the party to have a*

*quick chat to Airbnb to confirm that they had
indeed been partying?"*

Party city, Airbnb Hell

We've talked about how certain people with
the means have taken advantage of Airbnb's business
model to lease multiple units in a city and rent them
to Airbnb users at inflated prices. While this has led
to a decrease of available affordable housing in major
cities, it has also prompted officials to pass legislation
limiting stays of short-term renters. For example, in
New York, no Airbnb guest can stay longer than 30
days[5].

There are many reasons behind these laws,
most of which aren't designed to punish Airbnb users

---

[5] Fishman, J.D. Stephen. "Overview of Airbnb Law in New
York City." Nolo.com. N.p., n.d. Web.
<http://www.nolo.com/legal-encyclopedia/overview-
airbnb-law-new-york-city.html>.

but rather to prevent individuals from exploiting certain loopholes and drive up housing prices, and restrict certain tenants from being able to stay in a rental unless they're legally evicted[6]. However, one argument bystanders often overlook is the effect Airbnb rentals have on unsuspecting neighbors.

While as a perfectly normal and respectable Airbnb guest, you would think it would be your right to enjoy your vacation and celebrate with drinks and music, maybe even a small party for one night of your stay. That's hardly unreasonable if you don't cause any damage or leave a mess for the host, but think about how it affects permanent residents in

---

[6] Said, Carolyn. "Squatters Don't Sit Well with Airbnb Hosts." SFGate. N.p., 25 July 2014. Web. <http://www.sfgate.com/business/article/Squatters-don-t-sit-well-with-Airbnb-hosts-5631952.php>.

neighboring houses or apartments: no one asked them if it was alright to have people coming and going at all hours. Whereas a leaseholder might only have a noisy party once a month, an Airbnb apartment could potentially have one with each new guest.

> *"I just spent the last two nights in a nightmare! Actually it wasn't even a nightmare because I COULDN'T SLEEP! I rented a room on airbnb.com for the first time ever, and the crazy kids renting the room next to me were from Europe and didn't bother making the time adjustment, so they were literally up ALL NIGHT both nights smoking pot and blasting their music! I asked them to be quiet but they didn't... I asked the Host to give me a refund so I could go to a hotel, he said he would "talk" to the other guests, but nothing happened. Finally I contacted Airbnb and told them the story, and they ask me if I had any PROOF!! Right, I forgot to RECORD the crazy kids and try to document what time it was! Never using Airbnb again, seriously. It's just not worth it!"*
> Airbnb neighbors up ALL NIGHT, Airbnb Hell

Long-term renters, for better or worse, have certain habits. You can appeal to them if they're consistently loud. However, when there are different people occupying the property every few days of every week, it becomes an exercise in futility to complain. So too is trying to prove such noise occurred to Airbnb's customer service. Any ambient noise - cars, trains, machinery, cats in heat – can be written off as an unavoidable inconvenience in the area, but parties are more deliberate.

What can guests do when there is a party keeping them distracted or awake?

In this situation as in almost all of them, start recording. Provide a thorough account of your discomfort to provide to the Airbnb resolution center. Many representatives still might not give you a refund, which is why the best solution is often addressing the problem head on: confronting those

making the noise and asking them to stop; calling the

police; if hosts aren't directly involved, ask them to

step in. There are no guarantees.

> *"...the next morning I went to pick up my employee and you could just tell it had been a long night. The other guests stayed up until 5:00 AM partying, yelling at each other, banging on the windows, having guys over, drinking, eventually vomiting, and dry heaving until sunrise. It was not the sort of environment you would want to be in professionally. When you have to be up early and on camera all day, this room obviously wasn't going to work out.*
>
> *I called the host, explained the situation, and told him I was going to have to move my employee to ensure she was rested and ready to go to work. He understood but was apparently more concerned with the other guests? If I'm renting out rooms from my house I want to take care of the people that take care of my place. That was not the case here. So we agreed that he would refund half of the reservation and since that moment I haven't been able to get in touch with the host. I told him if he executed the refund process quickly I wouldn't make a big deal, wouldn't contact Airbnb, and wouldn't*

leave a nasty review even though he was owed
one for sure. A week went by and still nothing,
so I escalated the refund to Airbnb management.
They said they would be in touch. A few days
later (on Christmas morning at 10:00 AM) I
finally received an email from Airbnb saying the
case was resolved, and my request for a refund
had been denied. They couldn't reach the host to
verify my cancellation so they dismissed my
claim."

Airbnb Party House Open for Business, Airbnb
Hell

CHAPTER SIX: No matter what cancellation policy a host uses (strict, moderate, flexible), guests have little to no protection when hosts decide to cancel reservations at the very last minute. If you have to cancel your reservation at the last minute, the host has the right to keep some or all of your money for your entire stay.

First Scenario: If a host cancels on a guest at the last minute

> *"We spent a lot of time looking through listings, and found one that we thought was perfect. The host was well reviewed, and there were many positive comments. We paid the full amount and thought we were on our way. Fast forward to the night before we were to arrive. After several days of attempting to contact the host, she abruptly canceled our reservation with no warning and no explanation. We had only a few hours to find somewhere to stay."*
>
> <u>Last Minute Cancellation</u>, Airbnb Hell

Traveling can be one of the most stressful experiences

in someone's life. Leaving your home, even temporarily, means finding a place to sleep and store your belongings, searching for healthy food in a different area, and being safe when you don't know your way around... not to mention the hassle of waking up early, going through airport security, and dealing with delays and crowded spaces. A little preparation can go a long way towards alleviating the frustration behind these potential problems. However, when you think everything has been set in stone in terms of accommodations and arrive to find there is no place for you to sleep in this foreign city at night, or in the far reaches of the countryside where there are no hotels, calling the experience stressful is an understatement.

"I was traveling with my family (myself, my

wife, and my three-year-old daughter) in Los
Angeles where I had booked a nice cottage for
four nights. Everything was ok until the day of
our arrival at the host house. The same morning
I received a message saying she had to postpone
her departure and thus the house was not
available on the first night. Instead of cancelling
the booking she offered to book us a hotel room
for the first night at her expense. I obviously
accepted and started my trip to arrive there.
Later in the afternoon, around 5:00pm, just a
minute before arriving at her home (without any
news from the host about the hotel), I received a
cancellation notification from Airbnb.

The rest of the day was a nightmare. We found a
hotel for the night that cost a LOT more than the
Airbnb, but had a lot of problems booking it as
our credit card was maxed out due to the Airbnb
reimbursement not arriving promptly. Only in
the late evening did we get the money we needed
to let our daughter sleep in a hotel room instead
of a car... worst afternoon of my life..."
    <u>Airbnb Nightmare: Cancelled ONE MINUTE</u>
              <u>Before I Arrived</u>, Airbnb Hell

This is one of the biggest complaints from Airbnb

guests: hosts cancelling at the last minute, leaving

guests to either sleep in their cars or more than likely

book an expensive hotel room. Because no stay was completed, guests also do not have any ability to leave a review for the hosts, leaving others vulnerable to the same situation. Automated reviews are posted showing when the reservation was cancelled, but don't provide a reason or explanation.

What can guests do to protect themselves from flaky hosts?

Because last-minute cancellations do not allow Airbnb guests to leave reviews warning others of the hosts' behavior – it's possible their experiences were flukes and the host is not prone to cancelling, but how can anyone know? – there's very little preparation or research one can do to avoid flaky hosts. As of this writing, Airbnb has six different cancellation policies[7]:

1. **Flexible**. A full refund is allowed if notice is given 24 hours prior to arrival.

2. **Moderate**. A full refund is allowed if notice is given 5 days prior to arrival.

3. **Strict**. No full refunds are available. Guests may receive a 50% refund if they cancel one week prior to arrival.

4. **Super Strict 30 Days**. No full refunds are available. Guests may receive a 50% refund if they cancel 30 days prior to arrival.

5. **Super Strict 60 Days**. No full refunds are available. Guests may receive a 50% refund if they cancel 60 days prior to arrival.

6. **Long Term**. For Airbnb reservations

---

[7] "Cancellation Policies." Airbnb. N.p., n.d. Web.
<https://www.airbnb.com/home/cancellation_policies>.

exceeding 28 nights, a month's rent is paid to the host for any cancellation date prior to arrival.

While the penalties for guests cancelling a reservation are substantial, hosts have it much better. They are allowed one "free" cancellation for their first six months with no penalty, regardless of the length of the stay. They are charged a $100 fee if they cancel within a week of check-in, and $50 for anything beyond that[8]. This goes a long way towards explaining why hosts may simply be unconcerned with cancelling a reservation at the last minute; depending on the circumstances, they may incur no

---

[8] "I'm a Host. What Penalties Apply If I Need to Cancel a Reservation?" Airbnb Help Center. N.p., n.d. Web. <https://www.airbnb.com/help/article/990/i-m-a-host--what-penalties-apply-if-i-need-to-cancel-a-reservation>.

penalty for leaving a guest with a two-month reservation outside in the cold outside of having the dates blocked on their calendars.

For guests, the simple solution here is to not book a reservation via Airbnb unless they can afford to book a last-minute hotel room if necessary. During peak travel times, such as a large conference in a certain city for certain dates where all hotels are expected to be booked solid, guests would be better off avoiding Airbnb all together, or at least booking two or more simultaneous Airbnb reservations in order to improve their odds of having at least one place to stay if the other hosts cancel last minute.

> *"...I am writing here to warn people, as others have done, that Airbnb guarantees nothing. Their hosts can be complete flakes and cancel up to the last minute without suffering any consequences. Meanwhile, the guests, who've*

booked well in advance and paid in full, can be left in the lurch. It's fraud and I don't intend to let this go. This seems to be a frequent occurrence and is simply unacceptable. "
<u>Left in the Lurch After Host Cancelled on Short Notice</u>, Airbnb Hell

Second Scenario: If a guest cancels on a host at the last minute

Perhaps you've been fortunate enough to never be on the receiving end of a last minute cancellation, but what if you as a guest need to change plans or reschedule travel due to an emergency? Like many services, Airbnb does have a list of extenuating circumstances including death in the family, serious injury, natural disasters, extreme weather, property damage, and official restrictions in the event of a disease outbreak, jury duty, or political unrest in the area[9]. However, this is not an automated system: each reservation must be cancelled – leaving whatever payment was sent in limbo, subject to the same cancellation policies mentioned above – and then guests can contact Airbnb customer service to file a claim for a refund due to extenuating circumstances within two weeks. Whether this will be honored is another matter.

> *"My wife booked a house for our winter vacations in Lake Tahoe. The check-in time was at 3:00 PM. Around 1:00 PM an avalanche blocked the highway. We were 40 minutes away from the house and ready to go. However, we were asked to wait until the road would be accessible so we waited. The officers told us they would clean it up in a few hours but it kept raining and snowing; it was the biggest storm in the past decade. We had to drive back that night because there were no hotels available. I checked the news the next morning and the storm was even bigger; the road was blocked*

---

[9] "What Is Airbnb's Extenuating Circumstances Policy?" Airbnb Help Center. N.p., n.d. Web. <https://www.airbnb.com/help/article/1320/what-is-airbnb-s-extenuating-circumstances-policy>.

*for two days, so the only way to get to our
Airbnb reservation was with a helicopter.
Obviously, we didn't have one. Our host refused
to give us a refund. This is ridiculous; even
hotels and other Airbnb properties refunded
others. This was an extreme situation and it
wasn't fair our vacation got ruined. We lost our
money."*

Biggest Storm of the Decade not a Valid
Excuse, Airbnb Hell

The main flaw in Airbnb's business model is its

customer service department, woefully understaffed,

difficult to reach (see the "Other Useful Information"

appendix for Airbnb's contact number and email),

and full of representatives who have little to no

inclination to change anything outside of official

policy. Because most claims for refunds require

contacting Airbnb directly, there's no guarantee one

will be processed expediently, leaving guests

potentially short on cash and stuck in a different city

or town.

> *"Airbnb is great as long as nothing goes wrong. But the whole process is too complex for nothing to go wrong. In our case, we were not able to travel to our booking in Yosemite National Park because of a national weather service advisory about a winter storm which clearly mentioned "not to travel unless in an emergency". When we contacted Airbnb they suggested that we need to first cancel the booking and then claim a refund under their extenuating circumstances policy. After we cancelled the booking we filed a claim. The entire customer service experience was horrible. First of all, Airbnb could only be reached by email, which was slow. It took almost three days for Airbnb to reach a conclusion: they will not refund a single penny. When I asked for an escalation, a blunt email arrived stating that this was their final decision and they would not entertain any further communication."*
> Beware of Airbnb's Cancellation Policy, Airbnb Hell

Regardless, guests will never be refunded the service fee collected by Airbnb at the time of booking unless their extenuating circumstances claim is accepted, or the host cancels first.

SECTION II: HOSTS

CHAPTER ONE: If your guests claim any sort of insect/pest/vermin problem, Airbnb will instantly return 50% of your guests' money for their entire reservation, even if it's a year long reservation and the claim is false. This is a common scam tactic.

> *"This past month I had a seemingly nice couple staying with me in my condo… I saw the couple almost every day, talked with them, even drove them to the grocery store a few times! They NEVER had even the tiniest complaint about anything having to do with me or my condo. Well guess what, the day after they moved out I got a notice from Airbnb stating that the couple claimed they saw a MOUSE in the condo and that that Airbnb policy was to give them 50% of their money back FOR THE ENTIRE 4 WEEK STAY!!! Apparently the couple sent Airbnb a picture of a mouse… which I actually FOUND using a reverse search and Google! I sent Airbnb customer service numerous messages explaining that the incident was a huge lie and I even showed them the picture of the dead mouse the couple "saw" on another site that was posted over a year earlier! Airbnb took over a week to reply with a standard form email that simply said their policy was to supply a 50%*

refund."

Airbnb SCAM!, Airbnb Hell

Claims like this are what started the Airbnb Hell website, and made it less likely for hosts to accept long-term guests – not so much out of fear they would make a false report, but rather a simple risk analysis; if you have guests request several months or even weeks, anyone is capable of pulling this scam without facing consequences from Airbnb or the law.

> *"I had been a successful and enthusiastic Airbnb Host for almost a year when a young European couple in their mid 20's booked one of my rooms for a 6 month reservation, a very long stay by Airbnb standards. I welcomed them into my rental unit, and spent time with them socially on a few occasions during their stay as they were trying to learn their way around Los Angeles. My wife even sold them her used car well below blue-book value, just to help them out as they seemed like a nice young couple and they clearly didn't have a lot of money. Everything was going fine... until the couple left*

in the middle of the night without saying a word two nights before their 6 month reservation was scheduled to come to an end. I was surprised by that fact alone, but I was even more shocked when I received a notice from Airbnb saying that the couple had filed a complaint about me and they claimed there were mice in the condo! It should be noted that I had over 40 perfect reviews from previous guests at this point, and there most certainly were no mice anywhere on my property. According to Airbnb, their "standard policy" when a guest claimed rodents were in the house was to refund 50 percent of the entire reservation, in this case almost $3,000 USD for 3 months of renting one of my bedrooms in Los Angeles, California.

I immediately tried to contact Airbnb to dispute this obviously fraudulent claim, but I was passed around from one customer service agent to another, none of them able to give me any explanation better than "this is our policy". I was furious. After about 2 weeks of calling and emailing various Airbnb reps, I finally reached a "manager" who provided me with a copy of the scammers' complaint including a photo of a mouse they had sent. My rebuttal included written testimony from another guest who was staying in the condo at the same time, stating that there were no mice or signs of any other pests in the house. Thanks to the wonders of Google image search, I was even able to find

the exact same mouse photo that the couple had
used to file their complaint... it was originally
posted on a blog TWO YEARS EARLIER! I sent
all of this documentation to Airbnb and
asked them to consider my many positive
reviews, and that their "policy" to refund 50%
of a guest's entire reservation for a simple
(obviously fraudulent) claim was crazy.
Another week went by without my claim being
addressed. Airbnb kept my last payment from
the European scammers' reservation, as well as
money from my next few guests, so in total I had
lost almost $3,000."

Why Airbnb Hell Exists - From the Founder,
Airbnb Hell

What can hosts do to fight false accusations?

Aside from starting a website like

AirbnbHell.com so you can share your story with the

world, there's very little hosts can do once a claim of

mice or some kind of vermin has been filed with

Airbnb customer service within 24 hours of a stay.

However, despite the claims above and based on

many of the submissions to Airbnb Hell, the customer

service department seems to make completely arbitrary decisions on refunds for cockroach infestations and the like; many guests with legitimate claims appealed for refunds, only to be essentially told they were lying – e.g. "the host says there were no bedbugs" - or simply ignored. On the other hand, hosts with perfectly clean properties have had false accusations lobbed at them by guests with doctored pictures or photos of other properties. Some hosts have had limited success by getting written statements from other guests staying at a given property at the same time as the guest complaining of pests, but this often turns into a case of "he said, she said" so the resolution is usually for Airbnb to side with the guest in this scenario.

"I was so freaked out to hear that the guest had

abandoned the house that I thought something awful must have happened (like my cleaner forgot to prepare the house). I couldn't see the photos on my phone, and the representative I spoke to, "Colleen", chastised me and said that spiders don't spin webs overnight (actually, yes they do) so the house clearly was filthy enough to give her a refund. I asked why she didn't just turn around and leave upon arrival the day before if the place was so filthy, and Colleen had no answer for me. Colleen was so adamantly pro-guest and anti-host that if you told me that the scammer was her mother, that would be the only explanation for her bias that would make sense. Mind you, the scammer never called me, texted, or emailed me, my cleaner (who lives nearby), or my handyman at any time. This is how you know she is a scammer; she had no legitimate complaint and she didn't want to give anyone a chance to inspect or remedy anything that might be a genuine complaint."

Scammed by Guests, Airbnb Denies me Due Process, Airbnb Hell

CHAPTER TWO: If you make any claim regarding damage to reclaim part or all of the security deposit, Airbnb will make your life a living hell by demanding receipts for your original purchase even if it's furniture that you've owned for 20 years. If you don't have receipts, you're out of luck, and even if you do, it will take weeks or months to get any resolution.

> *"I rented my lovely Whistler townhome to someone who claimed to be a 27 year old coming up with his partner and another couple for a weekend to explore Whistler and the surrounding area. They were actually a group of at least 7 guys, probably younger than 27, who threw a big party at our quiet complex. There was evidence of cocaine, pot, cigarettes on top of the hundreds of beer cans and liquor bottles left behind – not to mention all the dirty underwear and various personal belongings they forgot. There was vomit on the curtains, cigarette butts and vomit on the balcony. Neighbors reported a loud party with a disco ball, loud music and women that appeared to be strippers/prostitutes. My cleaning lady told me she has never seen such a horrific mess in her 8 years of working in Whistler! My cleaning lady*

took 12.5 hours to clean my home, which normally takes 3 hours. Of course this came out of my pocket. Despite having photos of the mess and an invoice from my cleaning lady, Airbnb offered me no support and gave the guests' damage deposit back."

<u>Guests Trash Host's Townhome – No Support from AirBNB!</u>, Airbnb Hell

To the outside observer, Airbnb's policies don't even seem consistent. Guests can make claims that a host's lodging is dirty with little to no evidence and receive a 50% refund, but when a host offers more substantial proof that a guest has caused damage to his home, a whole slew of requirements are thrown down. No matter who is making the claim, it must be filed within 24 hours of a stay. For hosts, photographs or videos may simply not be enough to convince Airbnb's resolution center something has gone wrong.

"I had over $1500 in damage done by guests, all documented via photos and witnesses, and I even submitted professional estimates to repair walls, replace damaged dressers, sheets, mattresses, pillows, rugs, and carpet cleaning (guest took red lipstick and used it on my off white carpet all over the entire house!). I advised Airbnb at the VERY beginning of this guest abuse (verbal) that my house was being destroyed while they were here, it started slow and they went crazy with it when they departed (I was at work at that time). I was never given the option to evict them without penalties. I did EVERYTHING Airbnb asked of me from submitting the request to "guests" which was refused immediately by them along with NO denial that they did it, continued on with the representative who then told me I had to speak to a different team at Airbnb (this was now my FOURTH "pass off"). The new Airbnb individual said they needed documentation. I provided it and asked if he could access or if I needed to start from the beginning (I had A LOT of evidence so this was weeks worth of work), I also requested a number to call. The representative, Jake, said they have no number to contact them, that they would only offer "fair market value" (items are new and only 4 months old), and asked for additional/actual proof of original costs of the destroyed items. I searched emails and the web to find this after I told Jake I didn't have this information readily

accessible/available. No response. I email again
6 days later with everything ready and ask him
if what I have is what Airbnb needs, no
response. Airbnb appears to have closed the
claim…"
Guests Trash Host's Townhome – No Support
from AirBNB!, Airbnb Hell

That one million dollar host guarantee Airbnb throws

on its advertisements to entice new people to join?

It's virtually impossible to actually claim and seems

to be little more than a marketing ploy. Although this

policy is intended to reimburse for damages, it also

does very little in the event of theft.

> *"I decided to pop down to the shop to grab*
> *some groceries and when I came back about an*
> *hour later my bag was gone. And I don't mean a*
> *small bag. It was all my belongings I had*
> *brought with me. The host informed me that one*
> *of the guests had just left but she didn't notice*
> *what bags they had with them. We both spoke to*
> *Airbnb when I called to report it, and both of us*
> *got the same generic answer that without proof*
> *their hands are tied. What proof could I possibly*
> *have? A note from the thieves saying "Sorry, I*

stole your bag"?"
Airbnb guest stole my bag!!, Airbnb Hell

What can hosts do to get reimbursement for damages from Airbnb?

The official Host Guarantee from Airbnb lays down some requirements for hosts needing compensation from guests[10]. If there is a dispute for damages at a host's property, it's in the best interest of both parties to work it out amongst themselves. If that proves unsuccessful, a plethora of paperwork is required, including a police report for significantly damaged items, photographs of the damage, proof of ownership, and receipts for all of the damaged items. The company claims that if all these documents are

---

[10] "Host Guarantee Terms and Conditions." Airbnb. N.p., 27 Oct. 2016. Web.
<https://www.airbnb.com/terms/host_guarantee>.

submitted within two weeks of a guest's stay, then Airbnb customer service will have sufficient evidence to make a decision regarding who is at fault and if recompense is due.

> *"My roommate and I had a guest staying at our apartment for December break, since we were home visiting our parents. One guest in particular stayed on the 27th of December and decided to host a party. When I say party, I mean that the police were called multiple times, and we reached home two weeks later to find an eviction notice slapped to our front door due to multiple noise complaints. Since the maid service who had cleaned our apartment in between guests had only told us about damages in the apartment and the mess that it was left in, we were shocked to say the least. We went to the building manager to sort things out, and we were met with another surprise. The party that the guest had was not only loud and noisy, but her attendees were throwing things off the balcony, had broken the entry door as not all of them had the access key, and – here's the kicker – pooped on the stairwell outside our apartment.*

> *Airbnb had been contacted after the guests' stay as the maid service had informed us about extra*

cleaning charges, and so we emailed them again
telling them the new information. They gave us a
two-day extension to provide us with an invoice
for the damages. For those of you who have
never had to live in an apartment building with
a highly bureaucratic administration, you're so
lucky. For us, any little thing that has to be fixed
or replaced has to be reported to management,
who then has to file a maintenance order for it,
report it to their office who will then call a
company to take a look at the damage or assess
repairs, and then they will call another company
to do the actual repairs. The delay between each
of these communications is at least two days.

Added to this chain, there is a legal team who is
currently handling our file, as they are trying to
review what has to be paid for and if we should
pay for it. This team is not reachable by our
building office or by us; communication has to
go through the manager who will then ask them.
This adds another few days. I explained this to
Airbnb and they gave me another extension of
another two days. This went on for a week.
Finally, they emailed me saying I have 48 hours
and no more extensions. I have repeatedly gone
to the office and explained to them that I need
the invoice asap, but my urgency was probably
not conveyed to the legal team. When I emailed
the case manager and told him this he replied
saying that this is their protocol and he cannot
change it. He refused to connect me to a

71

*manager and said that there is no customer care
helpline I can connect with (I checked, there is).*

*Airbnb knows that we are helpless and is using
that to get out of paying for the damages caused
by that guest. The manager told me that
including the cleanup and everything, the
damages would amount to approximately $800,
maybe more. We cannot pay for this ourselves.
We're students; we were just trying to make up
a portion of our rent for the month that were
away. Most of it went towards a maid service
who cleaned the apartment between visits.
Airbnb has turned a blind eye to us, and emails
to the CEO have gone unanswered. We cannot
pay the amount in damages, and we are at our
wits end, missing classes to go talk to the
building manager, and staying up looking for
other channels of communication since our case
manager has shut the door in our face. We
cannot afford to start off a term like this, just as
we cannot afford to pay an insane amount for
absurd damages. Airbnb said that they would
commit to better service after their 2011
situation. But everything they had promised isn't
being held up by their representatives, and I
don't know what to do."*

Airbnb Refuses to Pay for Damages for Guest
Party, Airbnb Hell

The paperwork required for a damage claim is so extensive and may be a bureaucratic nightmare to obtain as in the aforementioned story, and even if everything is submitted on time and according to Airbnb's standards, there's no guarantee the claim won't be arbitrarily denied, leaving a host in debt for hundreds or thousands of dollars. Even if a claim is accepted, Airbnb can change the compensation to what they decide is best for both parties:

> *"We've determined that you should be compensated for your losses, however your guest has offered a higher amount than what we concluded would be the appropriate amount for the damages... I have gone ahead and processed this payout to your current preferred payout method."*
> <u>Airbnb Insurance for Damages is a Joke</u>, Airbnb Hell

This is another reason IKEA-furnished apartments are becoming so popular among professional hosts; with such cookie-cutter interior designs in housing they

only use for Airbnb, there's very little sentiment

attachment should a guest break a desk or cause water

damage. Hosts who are in fact renting out rooms or

their own home may want to consider a separate

insurance policy for their valuables as well as their

property.

CHAPTER THREE: Even if you use a Strict Cancellation Policy to protect yourself from flaky guests canceling their reservation at the last minute, Airbnb has the right to override that policy at any time and without warning or explanation and refund the guest the entire amount of their reservation, even if it's less than 24 hours before the guest is scheduled to check in.

"Two consecutive guests decided to cancel their booking at the last minute for medical reasons. (for two separate reservations); the second guest cancelled his booking days AFTER he was supposed to check in. In spite of us having a "strict" cancellation policy, Airbnb agreed to reimburse them for the full cost of their booking leaving us with an empty house at the last minute in the midst of the high season. To justify their decisions, Airbnb only sent us the link to their extenuating circumstances policy, which lists a very wide variety of circumstances left broad and vague on purposes. In this instance, given that both guests had emailed saying their cancellation was due to medical issues, we

asked Airbnb which objective criteria had been applied and the list of documents provided by guests to justify the fact they had to cancel at the last minute. In spite of our repeated queries, Airbnb refused to provide any objective criteria used to determine the circumstances of the cancellations. Of course they make these arbitrary decisions without losing any money themselves. Hosts end up losing money without having any say in the decision. These cancellations should be handled with a strict process similar to those applied by travel insurance policies. Hosts are NOT protected by Airbnb and this certainly doesn't feel like a community."

Airbnb Does NOT Respect Strict Cancellation Policy, Airbnb Hell

We've talked about how last-minute cancellations impact guests with an Airbnb booking; the only time they should be able to cancel without penalty is under extenuating circumstances as listed on the website[11]. While guests may not always be

---

[11] "What Is Airbnb's Extenuating Circumstances Policy?" Airbnb Help Center.

granted a full refund in these cases, hosts are just as vulnerable; having someone cancel at the last minute significantly reduces the odds of finding someone looking in the same area for the same dates. Airbnb may refund guests, but obviously the company has no desire to dip into their own profits to refund hosts.

"I've been an Airbnb host for four years with a total of 6 rooms for rent, so I've had hundreds of guests come and go, but I've never had an experience like this! Most of my rooms are rented several months in advance, and this case was no different. I had a nice couple message me a few months ago and ask to reserve my best room for a two-month stay, beginning August 24th (a few days from now). I agreed, and the reservation was made without any incident... until yesterday when I received a message from the guest saying that they had a "family situation" and they would have to cancel their reservation. I immediately replied and said I was very sorry to hear that, but that I would try to find replacement guests for their long term stay right away and that I would refund them for each night that I was able to replace them with other guests (even though I have always had a

STRICT cancellation policy set with Airbnb which entitles me to technically keep up to 100% of the guests money for up to one month if they cancel last minute like this). Granted I am a great host and have never actually taken a guests money or double-booked a room, but for the record I have that right when a guest cancels last minute. Well I never knew this was even possible, but somehow this guest contacted Airbnb directly and convinced them to OVERRIDE their own policy and my Strict Cancellation setting and give the guest a full 100% refund even though their move in date was only a few days away! How is that possible? What is the point of having a "Strict Cancellation Policy" with Airbnb if they can decide to override it at any time and completely screw one of their best and most loyal hosts?"

Airbnb Can Chose to Override STRICT
Cancellation Policy!, Airbnb Hell

What can hosts do to protect themselves from flaky guests?

When a host cancels a reservation on Airbnb, an automated review is posted showing the date of the cancellation. When a guest cancels a reservation, no review is posted, nor are any comments allowed.

While this makes it slightly easier for guests to determine how likely a host is to cancel, there's no data for hosts when considering whether to accept the booking of a guest. Because of this and the fact that there's no physical meeting between a host and guest prior to a stay, there's absolutely nothing a host can do if Airbnb decides a guest's reasons for cancelling fall under extenuating circumstances. This goes a long way in explaining why many hosts are hesitant about accepting guests without reviews; while Airbnb may have verified their identity and held their payment information, they can't guarantee certain guests aren't the type to cut and run.

CHAPTER FOUR: Airbnb has been known to cancel and remove even long-term hosts' listings without warning and without any explanation. This may cause you to lose communication with your current guests, and lose significant income for all upcoming reservations, which are also instantly canceled.

> *"We regret to inform you that, following a full review of your account, we have determined that we are unable to support your account on Airbnb. We have decided that it is in the best interests of Airbnb, and for the users on our site, to remove your profile from the Airbnb community.*
>
> *Additionally, we hope you understand that this decision is exercised at our sole discretion and that we are not obligated to provide an explanation as to the action taken against your account. Furthermore, we kindly note that we are not liable to a user in any way with respect to deactivating or cancelling his or her account.*
>
> *Additionally, please understand that this removal will also entail the immediate termination of your pending or accepted*

bookings and that, as part of this process, we will communicate to your host that the confirmed booking has been cancelled and the credit card used in this transaction will be fully refunded.

As per our Terms of Service, Airbnb reserves the right to make the final determination with respect to such matters, and this decision will not be reversed. We apologize for any inconvenience this may have caused and must inform you that, moving forward, we will no longer be able to assist you further with your account issue. We wish you all the best in your future endeavors. "

<u>Ban without explanation, did nothing wrong,</u>
Airbnb Hell

No explanation. No reason. Even we at

Airbnb Hell are just as confused as the unsuspecting

hosts. In some cases these account deactivations are

due to repeated violations of the terms of service, but

many hosts are claiming it's completely arbitrary:

"I have been a host on Airbnb for almost 4 years and in that time have bought some small rental units in a resort town to rent solely on

81

Airbnb as up until now it was the best platform and generated the most bookings. A few days ago I tried to log into my account to find that it had been deactivated for no apparent reason. Shortly after, I received an email with the usual Airbnb account termination paragraph stating that I had violated some term of theirs and a link to the TOA page which is 5 pages of rules long. I have only had good reviews and had hosted 300+ guests at my units, so there was no good reason I could think of why they would have done this to me. The least they can do in the situation is to offer you a reason so you can understand, and if necessary, defend your position. If that weren't bad enough, Airbnb also went ahead and cancelled $15,000 of upcoming reservations with no warning. I had some of the booked guests frantically call and email me as Airbnb cancelling on them was screwing them out of their vacation as the town was sold out of hotels and other vacation rentals and their trip was just a few days away. I had to explain how I had nothing to do with this and express my apologies and told them to contact Airbnb and ask them to reinstate the booking. They said they tried and that Airbnb just gave them the run around and showed no sympathy for their situation, even though they (Airbnb) were the ones who caused it. We ended up working out something on the side otherwise their vacation including flights etc would have had to be cancelled. Airbnb did however let the

82

current guests who were already in my units at the time of them closing my account stay but all of a sudden I could not communicate with the people occupying my property nor could they get in touch with me as my account was now closed. I complained to Airbnb saying by doing this it must be a violation of their own terms as denying communication to my guests and vice versa is not only dangerous but it is extremely poor customer service on their part. After 4 days I finally got a hold of the case manager assigned to my case and he apologized and said they screwed up and the situation was not handled correctly but they still were choosing to terminate my account anyway."

<u>AIRBNB CLOSED ACCOUNT -CANCELLED</u>
<u>$15k IN RESERVATIONS</u>, Airbnb Hell

I wish there were some methods Airbnb Hell could offer hosts and guests to prevent their accounts being deactivated but, as is the case with so many situations on Airbnb, there's little that can be accomplished. Even with the proper evidence of property destruction, claims for compensation are denied. When guests make false accusations against hosts, sometimes Airbnb provides refunds without a second thought. The decision to close someone's account seems to be just as irrational. Our best advice for Hosts using Airbnb is to also have hosting accounts setup in advance on competing sites such as <u>VRBO</u>, <u>HomeAway</u>, etc, so if your Airbnb hosting account is closed without warning, at least you might be able to quickly recover some revenue with reservations on other platforms.

<u>Other Situations on Airbnb</u>

Assault

Though there have been high profiles cases of assault and sexual assault from both hosts and guests[12], there is an underlying theme that makes such incidents all the more horrifying:

> *"I was sexually harassed and assaulted by a host I found on Airbnb. After the main incident, I escaped to my room, but I couldn't immediately leave the house because it was late at night and I had nowhere to go at that time, so I spent a terrifying night wondering if he would try to assault me again."*
> <u>Sexually Harassed by Host, Shameful Airbnb</u>

---

[12] Lieber, Ron. "Airbnb Horror Story Points to Need for Precautions." The New York Times, 14 Aug. 2015. Web. <http://www.nytimes.com/2015/08/15/your-money/airbnb-horror-story-points-to-need-for-precautions.html>.

When you're in a known environment – your home,

city, even country – and are the victim of sexual

assault, you would at least be familiar with the

emergency services and resources available to you:

the nearest hospital, the contact number for police, a

friend or family member to whom you can reach out,

and hopefully a safe place to stay. When you're

traveling abroad, nearly all these resources vanish.

> *"Even though I appreciated the empathy I received from Airbnb, I now feel, what can they really do if terrible things happened to me in that apartment in Bari, Italy? If I were in U.S. or even China, where I speak the language, I could have called the police immediately. I would also like to take legal action to the abusiveness this person demonstrated on me. But in a foreign country, without speaking the language, and Airbnb being the official party, who operates all the way on the east coast in the U.S. while real trauma was happening to me, what could they have done?"*

You cannot, nor should you, rely on Airbnb to help in a true emergency. Whether you're being attacked or simply fear for your safety as a host or guest, call the local authorities; do your research and find these contact numbers and locations before you depart. It can be scary to step out of a known situation like an Airbnb you booked online from the comfort of your home onto the streets of a foreign city, but there are always alternatives to staying with a host or guest who threatens you or makes you feel uncomfortable.

Racism

Airbnb Hell isn't responsible for the origin of #airbnbwhileblack stories, and there are few reports of racist behavior by hosts for one simple reason: Airbnb's business model allows hosts to view a guest's profile prior to accepting a stay. Though this was intended to reward guests with positive reviews and weed out those who tended to exhibit undesirable behavior in someone else's home, it has unfortunately been used at face value, literally; when hosts can see the profile pictures of those who request to stay, they can turn someone down simply because of his or her race. As a result, these incidents are very hard to prove: no reviews are allowed because no booking was made[13]. The only attempts to combat this serious problem have been the Instant Book option, in which

---

[13] Chandler, Adam. "Airbnb Challenges Its Hosts to Be Less Racist." The Atlantic, 08 Sept. 2016. Web. <http://www.theatlantic.com/business/archive/2016/09/airbnb-racism/499208/>.

hosts can offer available space to guests with immediate approval, and the company's new nondiscrimination policy[14]. These solutions fall short of addressing the underlying problem, and racial discrimination on Airbnb is still rampant[15].

Scams

> *"We messaged the number, got in touch with the host, and reserved the apartment. He asked us to do the payment through Western Union, which is generally a credible way to wire money, and so a week later we made a $700 payment ($300 for the apartment for three nights + $400 as a security deposit). We received confirmation emails from Airbnb as well and believed that everything was*

---

[14] "Airbnb's Nondiscrimination Policy: Our Commitment to Inclusion and Respect." Airbnb Help Center. N.p., n.d. Web. <https://www.airbnb.com/help/article/1405/airbnb-s-nondiscrimination-policy--our-commitment-to-inclusion-and-respect>.

[15] Greenfield, Rebecca. "Study Finds Racial Discrimination by Airbnb Hosts." Bloomberg. N.p., 10 Dec. 2015. Web. <http://www.bloomberg.com/news/articles/2015-12-10/study-finds-racial-discrimination-by-airbnb-hosts>.

confirmed. The payment was made to someone called Michael Harrison. The next day, the host reached out me and asked me to make another payment of $600; he said it was some sort of tax fee and that is when I realized something sketchy was happening."

My Airbnb Fraud Experience: Nightmare in

NYC, Airbnb Hell

When you're a guest making an Airbnb

booking, NEVER SEND MONEY TO SOMEONE

OUTSIDE THE WEBSITE. We've heard this story

so many times on Airbnb Hell with the same pattern:

1. Guest makes booking on Airbnb
2. Scammer suggests guest email him directly, or includes a link on his fake property listing
3. Scammer sends an official-looking email, which directs the guest to a fake Airbnb website
4. Guest enters credit card information and is told the system is down: a wire transfer is necessary
5. Guest sends money
6. Scammer sends fake email confirmation with Airbnb logos
7. Scammer stays in touch with guest as needed,

sometimes minutes before check-in

8. Guest arrives and finds nothing waiting

There are variations, of course, but nearly all include sending payment outside the Airbnb system. The host might be using a real address in your destination city, when he has no connection to it at all. Many of these scams have popped up in New York City, where visitors are desperate for affordable accommodations.

What should you do if you've been scammed? Unfortunately, Airbnb Hell has never heard of a case in which customer service actually provided a refund to someone scammed through their website. We're currently organizing a class action lawsuit for those who feel they have been cheated by Airbnb; please visit www.AirbnbHell.com to sign up.

Account Hacked

> *"A few weeks ago I received an email that my Airbnb account has changed. The hackers changed the email address (i.e. user ID) so I could not login. I had my credit card and driver's license and address and phone numbers, so they could adopt a kid using my identity. There was no way to contact Airbnb. No phone numbers, no email. After trying different ways, I signed up with a new email address and explained the situation. First, I received an automated email, which did not help at all. After reiterating the story, they corrected the situation, set my correct email address and gave me a temporary password. I logged into my account and to my horror I realized the hackers posted many phony listings for rent and discussed the prices etc with unsuspecting poor travellers. As an Airbnb user, I know that (most) property owners like to offer a direct deal to customers to avoid Airbnb charges. That means these guys probably got scammed with no traces on Airbnb."*
>
> <u>Security Breach</u>, Airbnb Hell

There have been cases of hosts' accounts being hacked, with the hacker filling in his bank account information to receive payment from unwitting guests. This is not a common occurrence, but Airbnb users should be mindful to log into their accounts every so often to confirm all their details haven't been modified.

Final Thoughts

So, is the situation hopeless on Airbnb? Are hosts always going to be vulnerable to scams and last minute cancellations, and are guests' fears about using the platform fully justified? While there certainly are a plethora of horror stories featured on Airbnb Hell, there are an even greater number of success stories in the forms of positive reviews and satisfied users.

If Airbnb made a serious commitment to change their business practices, we wouldn't be seeing the numbers of the former growing larger each day. One of the keystones of civil equality is access to public accommodations; in just a few short years, Airbnb has made that impossible in millions of rentals across the world by allowing hosts to secretly discriminate against racial groups and members of certain religions. However, hosts place themselves in financially precarious situations as well: every guest that steps through their doors has the potential to be a nightmare story involving theft, damaged property, and little if any remuneration from this so-called One Million Dollar Guarantee.

The company is starting to become more aware of the potential dangers facing hosts and guests, and how these problems can affect the value of the platform. Their non-discrimination pledge coupled with their recent ad campaign are attempts to soften the image of Airbnb without actually changing the process causing the problem in the first place. However, adding Instant Book and at least attempting to make it easier for guests to contact customer service is a step in the right direction.

Airbnb Hell never would have been created if it hadn't have been for the callousness of customer service and a business model that was particularly easy for unscrupulous guests to exploit. As difficult and impossible a task it may be, Airbnb needs to address these problems head on if they want to stay clear of lawsuits, conform to local laws, and provide a safe and trustworthy platform in the future. That means having a responsive and well-trained customer service center capable of delivering more than empty words and providing compensation where due. For others, it means having the support to get out of an uncomfortable or dangerous accommodation quickly without a litany of questions and paperwork.

Be aware when you travel, whether it's with Airbnb or even staying in a respectable hotel chain. All of the aforementioned problems aren't necessarily unique to Airbnb; rather, some come from simply living in an apartment complex, dealing with the trials and tribulations of traveling in a foreign country, and accepting that like any big business, the company isn't always capable of handling every crisis as it happens.

In summary, we at Airbnb Hell believe the "sharing economy" concept as a whole is here to stay, and overall it's having a positive impact on the world, however both Hosts and Guests using the Airbnb platform need to be aware of the risks and dangers associated with doing so, and should take steps to protect themselves as much as possible including

considering the use of Airbnb's Competitors

(http://www.airbnbhell.com/airbnb-competitors/).

Other Useful Information

How to contact Airbnb directly

The best toll-free phone number for calling Airbnb Customer Service is 1-855-424-7262 (Even with this number, the average wait time is between 7 and 12 minutes).

Another number that works well in the USA for local callers is: 1-415-800-5959

The way Airbnb prefers to be contacted is via their messaging center, here: https://www.airbnb.com/help/contact_us. Responses may take days or longer.

The primary Airbnb mailing address is:
888 Brannan St.
Floor 4
San Francisco, CA 94117

How to join Airbnb Hell's class action lawsuit

We're currently organizing a class action lawsuit to those who feel they have been cheated by Airbnb; please visit www.AirbnbHell.com to sign up.

How you can help

If you enjoyed this book and learned something new from it, we would deeply appreciate it if you would take a moment to give us a positive rating on whichever platform you used to purchase it!
If you would like to directly support us in our efforts to continue warning Airbnb Hosts and Guests, please visit http://www.airbnbhell.com/donations/airbnbhell-donations/ to make a donation.

Printed in Great Britain
by Amazon